CATALYST GARDENS

Where flowers and people grow

An Affirmation Coloring Journal
by Nicole B Roberts

This book belongs to

For inquiries, address:
nicole.the.creative.catalyst@gmail.com.

First edition published in the United States of America
October 2020
by
The Creative Catalyst LLC
www.TheCreativeCatalyst.Art

Dedicated to my paternal grandmother,

Rozella Broadhead

(1936-2017)

Like the flowers she loved,
she spent her existence quietly growing, always giving and
patiently enduring each season of life with a gentle,
but potent grace.

The most precious gift she ever gave me was her example.

Introduction

Each flower in this book symbolizes a positive
attribute that, if cultivated, will help us expand
our growth mindset.

When we meditate on the associated affirmation,
physically create a colorful symbol
and express our thoughts through journaling,
we are more likely to integrate the attribute
into our lives.

When we display the symbol
and share our thoughts with others,
we are planting little wisdom seeds.
We become a catalyst that creates a ripple effect!

When we make positive changes in ourselves,
we make positive changes in our world.
When we choose growth,
the universe follows our lead.

Sending love & light,

Nicole B Roberts

How to use this book

#1 On your own

Say the affirmation to yourself and contemplate
what it means as you color the picture.
Then, answer the prompt on the journal page.
Display your favorites where you can see them
as a reminder of the growth mindset
you are cultivating.

#2 With your family or friends

Create a growth mindset get-together.
Have each person pick which flower they are
drawn to, or put them face down and let people
pick at random.
Spend a few minutes doing the journal prompt.
Then, as you color your pictures, take turns
sharing your answers and discussing each
affirmation.
If you know each other well, take turns telling
others how they embody the affirmation they
received.

For more ideas, visit:

TheCreativeCatalyst.Art

WISDOM SEED

NOTHING

can dim the light that

SHINES

from within.

Maya Angelou

I am
OPULENT

The Orchid
is a symbol of luxury, beauty & opulence.

How can you grow in this area? How will you feel when you do?

"Beauty
begins
the moment
you decide
to be
yourself."

Coco Chanel

WISDOM SEED

LIFE

begins where

FEAR

ends.

Osho

I am
FAITHFUL

The Calla Lily

is a symbol of purity, holiness & faithfulness.

How can you grow in this area? How will you feel when you do?

"Faith
and fear
both demand
that you
believe
in something
you
cannot
see.
You choose!"

Bob Proctor

WISDOM SEED

Strive not to be a

SUCCESS,

but rather to be of

VALUE.

Albert Einstein

I am
WISE

The Iris
is a symbol of valor, hope & wisdom.

How can you grow in this area? How will you feel when you do?

"We don't receive wisdom; we must discover it for ourselves after a journey that no one can take for us or spare us."

Marcel Proust

WISDOM SEED

FREEDOM

lies in being

BOLD.

Robert Frost

I am
PURE

The Daisy

is a symbol of innocence, purity & new beginnings.

How can you grow in this area? How will you feel when you do?

"Experience, which destroys innocence, also leads one back to it."

James Arthur Baldwin

WISDOM SEED

GROWTH

is not a matter of

learning new information,

but

UNLEARNING

old limits.

Alan Cohen

I am
SENSITIVE

The Petunia
is a symbol of sensitivity, intimacy & companionship.

How can you grow in this area? How will you feel when you do?

"Your
sensitivity
is your
strength.
The way you
feel and love,
your
vulnerability
and
rawness--
that is
your power,
your purpose."

Marisa Donnelly

WISDOM SEED

Whatever makes you
UNCOMFORTABLE
is your
biggest opportunity
for
GROWTH.

Bryant McGill

I am
REFLECTIVE

The Pansy

is a symbol of nostalgia, free thinking & reflection.

How can you grow in this area? How will you feel when you do?

"Sometimes you will never know the value of a moment until it becomes a memory."

Dr. Suess

WISDOM SEED

It takes

COURAGE

to grow up and

BECOME

who you really are.

E.E. Cummings

I am
ENDURING

The Dahlia

is a symbol of enduring grace, elegance and inner strength.

How can you grow in this area? How will you feel when you do?

"What lies
behind us
and what lies
before us
are
tiny matters
compared
to what
lies
within us."

Ralph Waldo
Emerson

CHANGE

the way you look at things and the things you look at

CHANGE.

Wayne Dyer

I am
ABUNDANT

The Stargazer Lily
is a symbol of devotion, prosperity & abundance.

How can you grow in this area? How will you feel when you do?

"Abundance
is not
something
we acquire.
It is
something
we tune
into."

Wayne Dyer

It always seems

IMPOSSIBLE

until it's

DONE.

Nelson Mandela

I am
TENACIOUS

The Columbine

is a symbol of fortitude, courage & tenacity.

How can you grow in this area? How will you feel when you do?

"Some succeed because they are destined to, but most succeed because they are determined to."

Henry Van Dyke

WISDOM SEED

AWAKENING

*is not discarding
who you are,
but discarding who*

YOU

are not.

Deepoak Chopra

I am
ENLIGHTENED

The Lotus
is a symbol of self-regeneration, rebirth & enlightenment.

How can you grow in this area? How will you feel when you do?

"Sometimes you have to lose yourself to discover who you might yet be. Sometimes what feels like breaking down is really just breaking free."

Cristen Rodgers

EVERYTHING

you ever wanted is on the other side of

FEAR.

George Addair

I am
FEARLESS

The Daffodil
is a symbol of rebirth, new beginnings & fearlessness.

How can you grow in this area? How will you feel when you do?

"And
suddenly
you know:
It's
time
to start
something
new
&
trust
the magic of
beginnings."

Meister Eckhart

I have no special talent,
I am only

PASSIONATELY
CURIOUS.

Albert Einstein

I am
PASSIONATE

The Rose

is a symbol of love, passion, confidentiality.

How can you grow in this area? How will you feel when you do?

"The
most
powerful
weapon
on earth
is the
human soul
on fire."

Ferdinand Foch

Adopt the pace of

NATURE

her secret is

PATIENCE.

Ralph Waldo Emerson

I am
TRANQUIL

The Poppy

is a symbol of sleep, peace & tranquility.

How can you grow in this area? How will you feel when you do?

"When
we are
unable
to find
tranquility
within
ourselves,
it is
useless
to seek it
elsewhere."

La
Rochefoucauld

JOY

is the evidence of

inner

GROWTH.

Maria Montessori

I am
JOYFUL

The Sunflower
is a symbol of loyalty, longevity & joy.

How can you grow in this area? How will you feel when you do?

"Joy
is a
decision,
a really
brave
one,
about
how you are
going to
respond
to life."

Wess Stafford

WISDOM SEED

Life shrinks or

EXPANDS

in proportion to ones

COURAGE.

Anais Nin

I am
PROSPEROUS

The Hibiscus
is a symbol of glory, fame & prosperity.

How can you grow in this area? How will you feel when you do?

"Prosperity
starts
in ones
heart
not
their
pocket."

Ricky Maye

In a

GENTLE

way, you can

SHAKE

the world.

Mahatma Gandhi

I am
CHARMING

The Ranunculus
is a symbol of attractiveness, charisma and charm.

How can you grow in this area? How will you feel when you do?

"Charisma is a sparkle in people that money can't buy. It's an invisible energy with visible effects."

Marianne Williamson

CHANGE

is inevitable

GROWTH

is optional.

John Maxwell

About the Creator

Nicole B Roberts

is a self-taught artist, an author,
and a free-spirited creator
attempting to gracefully raise three wild offspring while
chasing her bearded husband
on his oilfield adventures in Midland, TX.

Raised beneath the mountains in West Jordan, UT by an
outdoorsman/ book salesman and an artist/ elementary
school teacher likely sparked her lifelong love of learning.

She is ever inspired by nature, color, cycles, symbolism,
growth, finding the good in people, authenticity,
vulnerability, the magic of words
and above all, love.

Her purpose in all she does is to model and reiterate that we
were each "created to create"
and that our joy is hiding within
the acceptance of that divine identity.

You can see which creative squirrels she is chasing next at:

TheCreativeCatalyst.Art

Connect & Share

Be a part of our High Vibe Tribe!
We would LOVE to see your creations and hear about
your experience with this book.

@the.creative.catalyst

facebook.com/
thecreativecatalyst

@the.creative.catalyst

#thecreativecatalyst
#catalystgardens

TheCreativeCatalyst.Art

www.ingramcontent.com/pod-product-compliance
Lightning Source LLC
Chambersburg PA
CBHW080602030426

42336CB00019B/3301